Gravity-Defying Animals

Animals with Super Powers

by Natalie Lunis

Consultants:

Robert Dudley, PhD
Professor and Director, Animal Flight Laboratory
University of California, Berkeley

Jake Socha, PhD
Assistant Professor
Department of Engineering Science and Mechanics
Virginia Tech

BEARPORT
PUBLISHING

New York, New York

Credits

Cover and Title page, © McDonald Wildlife Photography/Animals Animals–Earth Science; Cover TR, © Cheri131/ Dreamstime; 4L, © Ainars Aunins/Shutterstock; 4R, © David Osborn/Alamy; 5T, © Ivy Photo/Shutterstock; 5B, © Daniel Hebert/Shutterstock; 6, © Evgeniya Urarova/Shutterstock; 6–7, © Keneva Photography/Shutterstock; 7R, © Daniel Prudek/ Shutterstock; 8–9, © Anton Sokolov/Shutterstock; 9T, © Christian Hatter/Imagebroker/FLPA; 10–11, © NHPA/Photoshot; 11, © Picstudio/Dreamstime; 12, © Steven Russell Smith Photos/Dreamstime; 13, © McDonald Wildlife Photography/ Animals Animals–Earth Science; 14, © JoeFotoSS/Shutterstock; 15, © Cede Prudente/Photoshot; 16, © Wildlife GmbH/ Alamy; 17, © Waterframe/Alamy; 18, © Microscan/Phototake Inc/Alamy; 19, © Yuttasak Jannarong/Shutterstock; 20, © CreativeX/Shutterstock; 21, © Ann Hough/National Elk Refuge/USFWS; 22T, © Steve Byland/Shutterstock; 22B, © DDCoral/Shutterstock; 23, © Craig Dingle/iStockPhoto.

Publisher: Kenn Goin
Editorial Director: Adam Siegel
Creative Director: Spencer Brinker
Design: Dawn Beard Creative
Photo Researcher: Brown Bear Books Ltd

Library of Congress Cataloging-in-Publication Data

Lunis, Natalie.
  Gravity-defying animals / by Natalie Lunis.
     pages cm. — (Animals with super powers)
  Includes bibliographical references and index.
  ISBN 978-1-62724-080-2 (library binding) — ISBN 1-62724-080-2 (library binding)
  1. Animal locomotion—Juvenile literature. 2. Flight—Juvenile literature. I. Title.
  QP311.L86 2014
  591.5'7—dc23
                          2013029545

For more information, write to Bearport Publishing Company, Inc., 45 West 21st Street, Suite 3B, New York, New York 10010. Printed in the United States of America.

10 9 8 7 6 5 4 3 2 1

Contents

Defying Gravity

Gravity is an invisible yet powerful **force**. It pulls people, animals, and objects down to the ground so that they don't float into the air. From children racing down a snowy hill to leaves falling from a tree, gravity is always acting on people and on everything around them.

Ruby-throated hummingbird

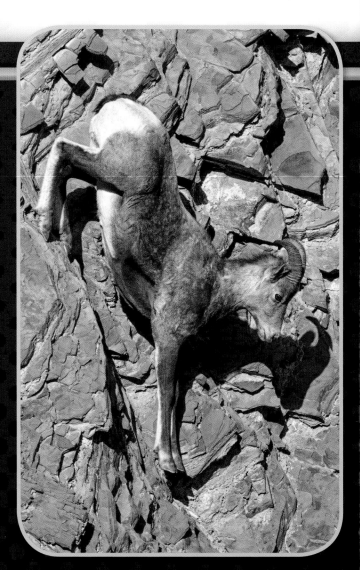

Bighorn sheep

As powerful as gravity is, there are certain animals that **defy** it every day. Some do so by flapping their wings to fly incredibly high. Others shoot out from under the water. Still others stick to the ceiling without any glue. In this book, you will read about eight of these extraordinary creatures—and the secrets behind their gravity-defying powers.

Tokay gecko

Bar-headed
geese

Hummingbird

Most kinds of birds can fly. However, only one kind can **hover**—staying in one place in the air—for more than a few seconds. This unusual flier is the hummingbird.

How does being able to hover help the hummingbird? It gives it the power to stop and feed on a flower's **nectar** while staying in midair. When it is done eating, the tiny bird zooms off to find more fuel for its body. It might visit up to 1,000 flowers a day to feed on nectar!

When it is not hovering, the hummingbird shows its other special talent. In addition to being able to zip forward, upward, and downward, it can fly backward. That's something else no other bird can do.

There are more than 300 kinds of hummingbirds. They live in many parts of North America, Central America, and South America.

Hummingbirds are small. Some are only two inches (5 cm) long and weigh only as much as a penny. Their long, thin bills help them reach the nectar in the center of flowers.

bill

Hummingbirds get their name from the humming sound that is made by their fast-moving wings. These wings can beat up to 80 times per second.

The only insects that can hover well are different kinds of bees, wasps, and flies. Like hummingbirds, they feed on nectar from flowers—as well as on powdery pollen.

Bar-Headed Goose

About one third of the world's bird **species migrate**. Every year, these migrating birds fly from summer homes, where they nest and lay eggs, to winter homes, where they find warmer weather and food, and then back again. Some of the journeys are fairly short, while others cover hundreds and sometimes even thousands of miles. Still others take place at amazing heights above the ground.

The bar-headed goose flies higher than any other bird when it migrates. Every fall and spring, flocks of bar-headed geese pass over the snow-covered Himalaya Mountains—the world's tallest **mountain range**. While doing so, they have been known to reach heights of more than 21,457 feet (6,540 m). Some people have even reported seeing the geese flying over Mount Everest, the world's highest mountain.

The Himalaya Mountains are in southern Asia.

The upper part of Mount Everest is a very dangerous place. No plants or animals are able to live there because of extremely cold temperatures, powerful winds, and air that has much less **oxygen** than the air in lower-lying parts of the planet.

The bar-headed goose gets its name from the black bars on its head.

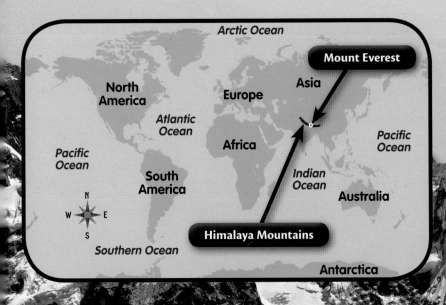

Arctic Ocean

Mount Everest

North America

Europe

Asia

Atlantic Ocean

Pacific Ocean

Africa

Pacific Ocean

South America

Indian Ocean

Australia

N
W   E
S

Himalaya Mountains

Southern Ocean

Antarctica

Bat

All over the world, flying birds and insects rule the skies. There is only one kind of **mammal**, however, that shares the air with them. Like these birds and insects, it flaps its wings and uses muscle power to control its direction and speed. This flying animal is the bat.

While bats have large, strong wings for flying, most kinds have very weak legs. It is hard for them to stand up or walk on them. They also can't run fast enough to take off from the ground. As a result, when bats are not flying, they hang upside down from branches or rocks in caves. When it's time to fly, they let go, drop into the air, and flap away into the night.

There are more than 1,200 species of bats. They live in all parts of the world except the very coldest— the Arctic and Antarctic.

Like almost all mammals, bats have fur on their bodies. Their wings, however, are covered with smooth, stretchy skin— and just a few hairs.

Hanging high up helps bats stay safe from cats, foxes, and other animals that might catch and eat them on the ground.

Flying Squirrel

In spite of its name, a flying squirrel doesn't truly fly. That's because it doesn't have flapping wings that it can move up and down. Yet the small mammal certainly seems to fly from tree to tree in the forests where it lives. How does it pull off this gravity-defying trick?

Instead of flying, the squirrel **glides** by using large flaps of skin on its sides to catch air and keep itself from dropping straight down. To take off, it climbs high up in a tree and jumps—opening its front and back legs to stretch the skin in between. The squirrel then sails through the air on a slightly downward path before coming in for a landing.

There are about 50 species of flying squirrels. They live in forests in North America, Europe, Africa, and Asia.

Flying squirrels move around only at night. They look for many different foods—including berries, nuts, insects, and mushrooms—both in trees and on the ground.

While it is gliding, a flying squirrel can use its body to steer either straight ahead or to turn.

Flying Snake

Snakes are **reptiles** that have long, thin bodies with no legs. As a result, to get from one place to another, they have to crawl on their bellies—or do they?

In forests in Southeast Asia, a few kinds of snakes—known as flying snakes—appear to fly from tree to tree. When one of them is ready to take off, it crawls to the end of a branch. The snake then flattens its body—becoming twice as wide as it was before—and pushes off. As it sails through the air, it bends its body from side to side in quick, wave-like movements. Why do these snakes travel this way? No one is sure—but it's clearly faster than creeping all the way down to the ground and back up again!

There are five different species of flying snakes. They are from two feet to four feet (.6 to 1.2 m) long.

Flying snakes hunt for food during the day. They catch and eat mainly lizards, as well as a few birds and bats.

A flying snake does not really fly. Instead, it glides. Like other gliding animals, it moves from a higher point to a lower point as it travels through the air.

Flying Fish

Flying fish don't really fly. However, that's what they seem to do when they pop out of the ocean at high speed and spread their side **fins**. The fins act like wings, catching the air and lifting the fish over the water. Sometimes the unusual creatures shoot up as high as four feet (1.2 m) or more above the surface.

Why do these fish defy gravity and take to the air? Their daring tricks actually help them stay safe. In oceans around the world, they are eaten by dolphins, sharks, tuna, and other fast swimmers. Speeding up underwater and then taking a gliding leap is a quick and tricky way to escape these powerful **predators**.

Flying fish live mainly in warm ocean waters. Sometimes they travel in large groups called schools.

There are about 40 species of flying fish. They measure from 6 to 18 inches (15 cm to 46 cm) in length.

Sometimes a flying fish makes several gliding leaps in a row.

Gecko

Geckos are small- to medium-size lizards that have not just one, but a few different superpowers. They can lick their eyeballs to keep them clean. They can grow a new tail if the one they have breaks off. Most impressively of all, they can defy gravity in a way that few other animals can.

Every kind of gecko can walk on walls and ceilings. The surfaces they stick to can even be smooth and slippery—for example, glass windows and doors. How do the lizards hang on? Using the world's most powerful microscopes, scientists have found the answer. At the bottom of a gecko's foot are millions and millions of tiny hair-like strands that split into even more tiny ends. The strands work together to form a **bond** with whatever surface the lizard walks on—a bond so strong that it keeps the gecko from falling off.

A close-up photo showing the tiny hairs on a gecko's foot

There are about 1,500 species of geckos. They live in warm places all over the world.

Other animals with different kinds of feet, including spiders, flies, and tree frogs, can also walk on walls and ceilings. However, at up to 14 inches (35 cm) in length, the gecko is the largest animal that can do so.

Bighorn Sheep

Rock-climbing requires both skill and courage. In this daring sport, climbers—who often wear or carry special gear—attempt to reach the tops of steep, rocky cliffs. Then they must carefully get themselves back down.

Among animals, some of the best and most fearless rock climbers are bighorn sheep. Of course, these high-climbing animals don't use any gear, but they do have something that helps them hang on— their feet. The outer part of a bighorn sheep's foot is a tough **hoof** that is shaped in a way that is good for grabbing onto rough spots. The middle part is made up of a rubbery pad that grips smooth surfaces. Thanks to these body parts, the sheep is able to do some very fancy footwork—and outclimb predators that roam the mountainsides.

Bobcats, coyotes, and wolves are some of the animals that hunt bighorn sheep.

bobcat

Bighorn sheep are found in western North America and northern Asia. They live in the desert as well as mountainous areas.

Mountain goats have feet that are built in a similar way. Like bighorn sheep, they are world-class climbers.

More About
Gravity-Defying Animals

○ Like bats, hummingbirds have weak legs and cannot walk on the ground. When they sleep, they perch upright on a branch.

● People who drive on highways in places where flying squirrels live can sometimes see the animals gliding across the road at night. However, they usually think they are seeing birds flying instead! Flying squirrels can glide up to 150 feet (46 m) through the air.

○ Scientists are studying the feet of geckos in order to try to come up with new inventions. These include super-sticky tape and robots that can walk up walls.

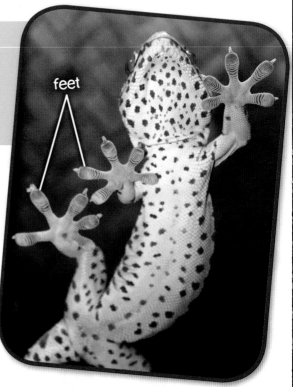

feet

● In ancient Greece, people often saw flying fish jumping out of the water at night. As a result, they mistakenly thought that the fish left the water to sleep on land.

Glossary

bond (BOND) the sticking together of one thing to another

defy (dih-FYE) to resist

fins (FINZ) flap-like body parts that fish and other animals use to steer while swimming

force (FORSS) something that causes movement, such as a pull or push

glides (GLYEDS) to travel through the air by moving from a higher place to a lower place

gravity (GRAV-uh-tee) the force that pulls things toward the ground and keeps them from drifting into the air

hoof (HUF) a hard covering on the foot of an animal, such as a sheep or horse

hover (HUHV-ur) to stay in one place in the air

mammal (MAM-uhl) a warm-blooded animal that has a backbone, hair or fur on its skin, and drinks its mother's milk as a baby

migrate (MYE-grate) to move from one place to another at a certain time of the year

mountain range (MOUN-tuhn RAYNJ) a group of mountains that are close together

nectar (NEK-tur) a sweet liquid found in flowers

oxygen (OK-suh-juhn) a colorless gas that is found in the air and water and that animals and people need to breathe

predators (PRED-uh-turz) animals that hunt and kill other animals for food

reptiles (REP-tyelz) cold-blooded animals, such as lizards, snakes, turtles, or crocodiles, that use lungs to breathe and usually have dry, scaly skin

species (SPEE-sheez) groups that animals are divided into according to similar characteristics; members of the same species can have young together

Index

Bibliography

Alexander, David E. *Why Don't Jumbo Jets Flap Their Wings? Flying Animals, Flying Machines, and How They Are Different.* New Brunswick, NJ: Rutgers University Press (2009).

Godkin, David. "How Bar-Headed Geese Scale the Himalayas." *Scientific American* (November 2011). http://www.scientificamerican.com/article.cfm?id=olympians-of-the-sky

Logan, William Bryant. *Air: The Restless Shaper of the World.* New York: W. W. Norton (2012).

Read More

Bishop, Nic. *The Secrets of Animal Flight.* Boston: Houghton Mifflin (1997).

Branley, Franklyn M. *Gravity Is a Mystery.* New York: HarperCollins (2007).

Mullins, Matt. *Gravity.* New York: Children's Press (2012).

Simon, Seymour. *Ride the Wind: Airborne Journeys of Animals and Plants.* San Diego, CA: Browndeer Press (1997).

Learn More Online

To learn more about gravity-defying animals, visit
www.bearportpublishing.com/AnimalswithSuperPowers

About the Author

Natalie Lunis has written many science and nature books for children. She lives in the Hudson River Valley, just north of New York City.